I am so 4 !

Sky Pony Press books may be purchased in bulk at special discounts for sales promotion, corporate gifts, fund-raising, or educational purposes. Special editions can also be created to specifications. For details, contact the Special Sales Department, Sky Pony Press, 307 West 36th Street, 11th Floor, New York, NY 10018 or info@skyhorsepublishing.com.

Sky Pony® is a registered trademark of Skyhorse Publishing, Inc.®, a Delaware corporation.

Visit our website at www.skyponypress.com.

Authors, books, and more at SkyPonyPressBlog.com.

10 9 8 7 6 5 4 3 2 1

Library of Congress Cataloging-in-Publication Data is available on file.

Cover illustration and design by John Kurtz

Print ISBN: 978-1-5107-4511-7
Ebook ISBN: 978-1-5107-4514-8

Printed in China

I am so 4!

LOOK AT EVERYTHING I CAN DO!

Sandrina and John Kurtz

Sky Pony Press
New York, New York

I can put my
own shoes on,

and skip around outside.

I can swing,

and kick a ball.

I can listen to stories,

and tell you how I feel.

Happy

Sad

Hungry

Afraid

I can have a tea party,

and wash dishes.

I can peel
a mandarin
orange,

and go berry picking.

I can make a
puppet show,

and play board games.

I can draw
my family,

and use safety scissors.

I can string beads,

and use finger paints.

I can play dress-up,

and dress my friend up too!

I can play catch with my dog,

and share a snack.

I can hop on
one foot,

and do a somersault.

I can wash
my hands,

and brush my teeth.

I can pedal
my tricycle,

and climb a ladder.

I can draw different shapes,

and bake cookies.

I can be polite
and say, "Please," and, "Thank you."
I can do all these things and more,
because I am so four!

Please

Thank you